MEANWHILE, BACK IN MEDILAND...

THAT POOR CUTE, CUTE, BOY!

COME ON, LET'S FIND THE OTHERS. WE'VE GOT WORK TO DO!

MMM...TOASTY.

HEY GASTRO--HAVE YOU SEEN MY PLASMA TORCH ANYWHERE?

WHAT'S THE MEANING OF...?

MY TOOLS!

THE TRICK IS TO HEAT THE MARSHMALLOW SLOWLY, SO THE CENTRE GETS GOOEY WITHOUT THE SUGARY DELICIOUS EPIDERMAL LAYER BLACKENING.

MMM... BLACKENING.

HEY, AREN'T YOU SUPPOSED TO BE ON WATCH!?!

WHAT ARE YOU DOING IN HERE?

WHAT WE DO EVERYDAY.

TRYING TO TAKE OVER THE WORLD!

SORRY. COULDN'T RESIST. TOASTED MARSHMALLOW?

MY PERFECT, BEAUTIFUL TOOLS...

UH-OH, BOYS. HIS VEIN IS POPPING.

EARS STEAMING.

HE'S GONNA BLOW!

THEY'RE RUINED. RUINED!

MEDI-MIGHT GO! I HAVE SUPERHUMAN STRENGTH

MEDI-MORPH GO! I CAN MORPH INTO A SKELETON!

MEDI-VISION GO! MY GLASSES DOUBLE AS A MEDI-SCOPE!

MEDI-GAS GO! I CAN PROPEL MYSELF THROUGH MEDILAND WITH MY WORLD FAMOUS FARTS!

MEDI-TATE GO! I CAN HELP YOU RELAX.

OUR SUPER-POWERS LET US KNOW EVERYTHING ABOUT HOW THE BODY WORKS... ESPECIALLY ME.

...AND ME

AND YOU'RE HERE BECAUSE...?

WE'RE GOING TO TEACH YOU EVERYTHING YOU NEED TO KNOW ABOUT YOUR *SCOLIOSIS.*

IT'S NOT COOL TO FIND OUT YOU HAVE SCOLIOSIS, BUT IT HELPS IF YOU UNDERSTAND IT.

AND YOU CAN FORGET THE TEXT-BOOK. WE DO THINGS DIFFERENTLY AROUND HERE.

WE ARE GOING TO TAKE YOU ON A FANTASTIC VOYAGE.... TO A GIANT LIVING PLANET SHAPED LIKE THE *HUMAN* BODY!

OUCH! THAT'S TWICE!

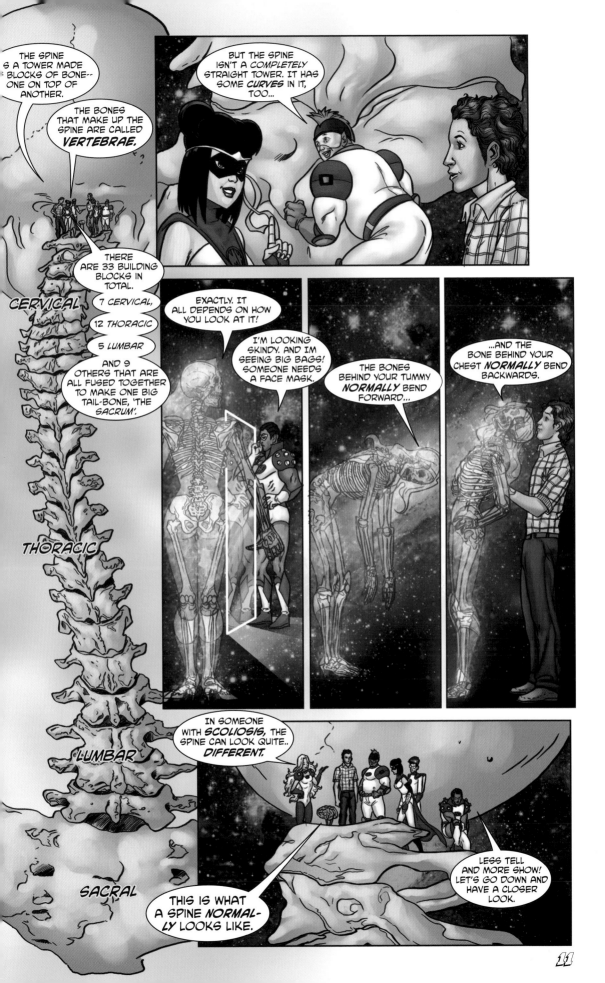

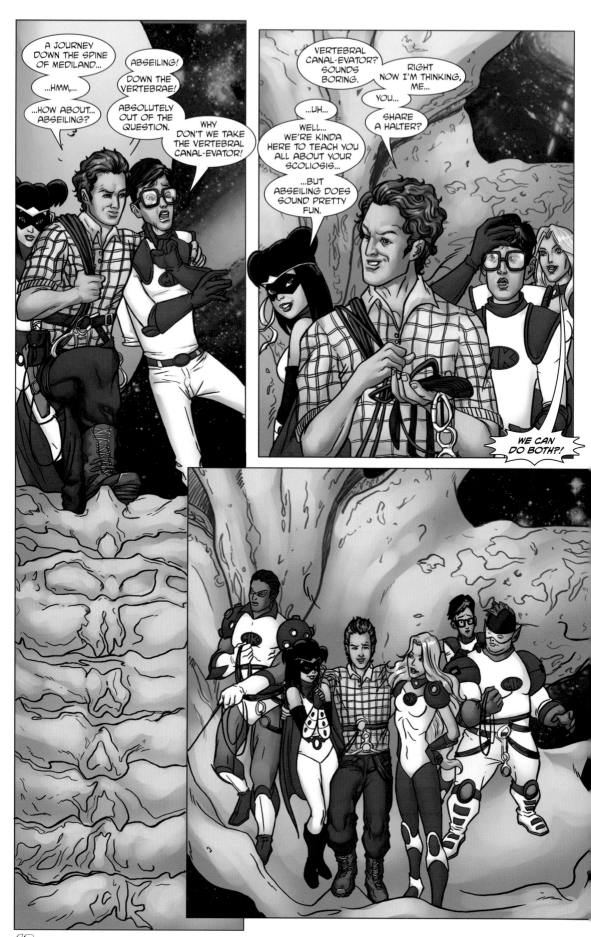

12

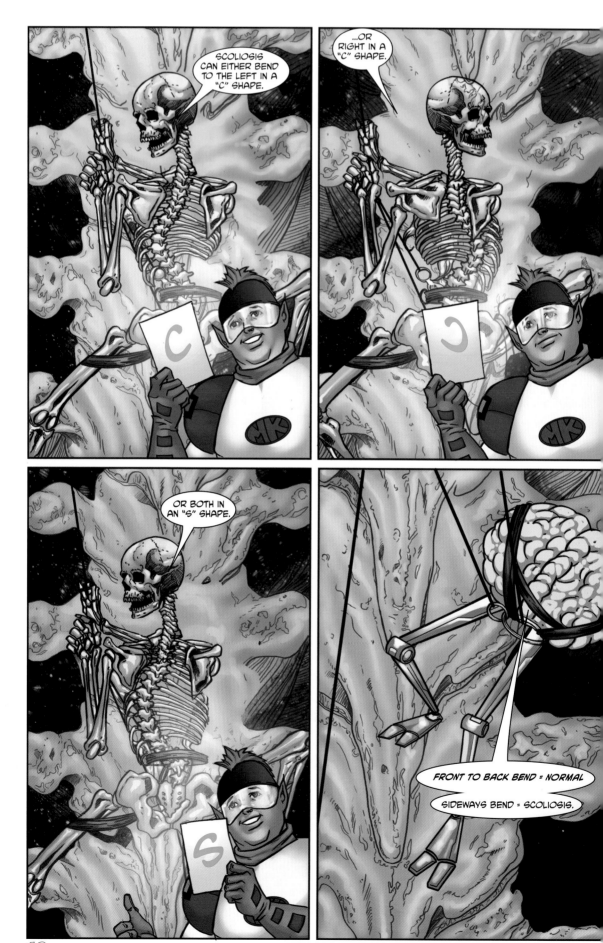

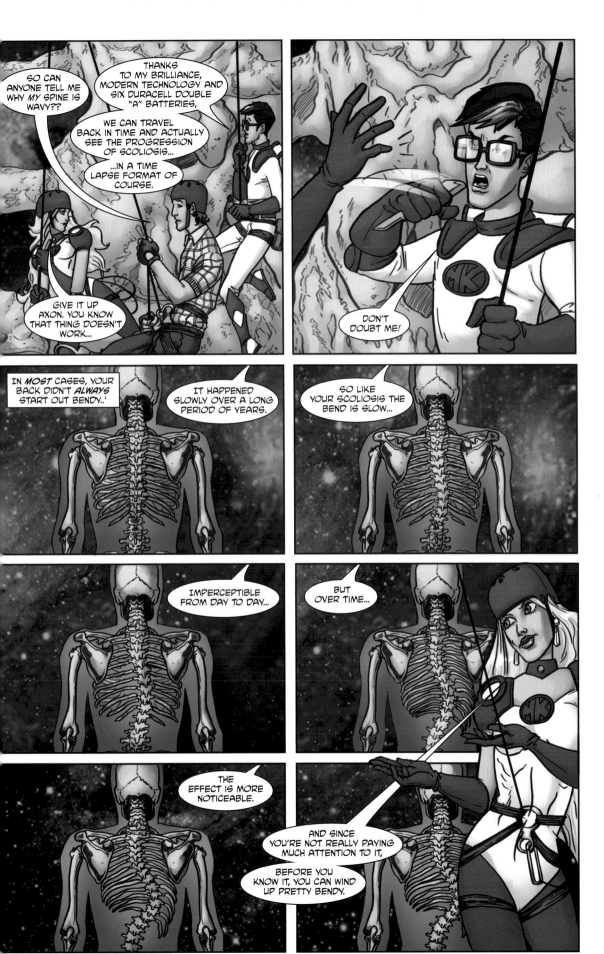

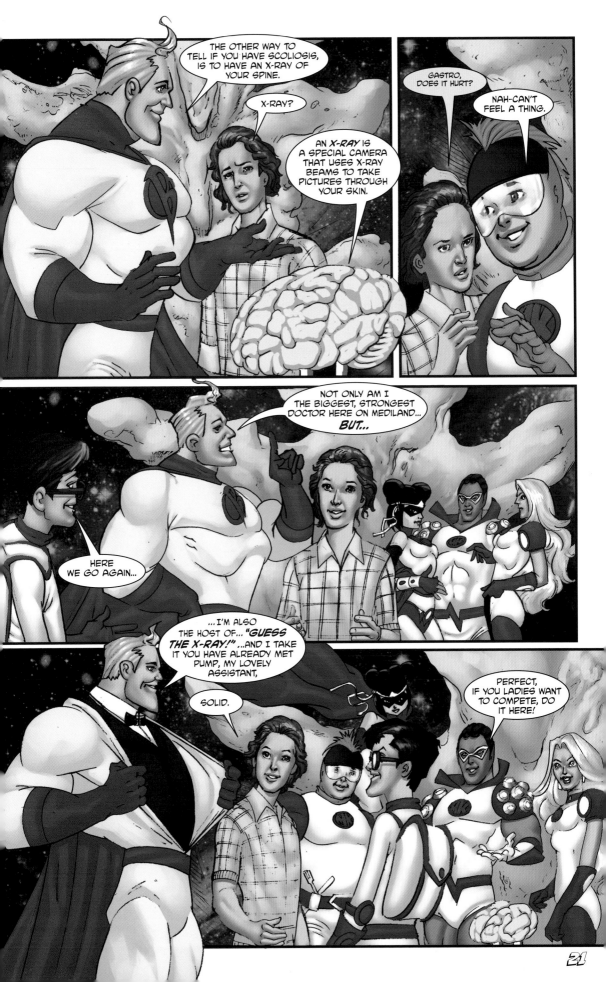

AM I GOING TO BE COOL?

JOHN--YOU OOZE COOL.

NO, I MEAN THE *SCOLIOSIS*? IS THIS SERIOUS?

LET'S SEE. WE MEASURE THE BEND BY DRAWING LINES AND MEASURING ANGLES ON YOUR X-RAY PICTURES. IF THE BEND IS LESS THAN 20 DEGREES, YOU MAY NOT NEED ANY TREATMENT.

THE YOUNGER YOU ARE, THE MORE IMPORTANT IT WILL BE FOR THE DOCTOR TO WATCH OUT, BECAUSE YOU HAVE A LOT OF GROWING TO DO.

IF THE CURVE IS BETWEEN 20 - 30 DEGREES, YOU MIGHT NEED TO WEAR A BRACE.

AND IF IT'S MORE THAN 45 DEGREES - YOU MIGHT NEED SURGERY TO STRAIGHTEN YOUR BACK OUT.

THESE ARE JUST GENERAL BALL-PARK FIGURES THOUGH. BRACING OR SURGERY IS DONE WHEN WE THINK THERE *MAY* BE A PROBLEM IN THE FUTURE. WE WATCH AND WAIT - JUST LIKE YOU WATCHED MEDILAND DEVELOP BEFORE YOUR EYES, AND IF IT LOOKS LIKE IT MAY BEND TOO MUCH, THEN YOU MIGHT NEED US TO INTERVENE. UNTIL THEN, WE WILL JUST KEEP AN EYE ON THINGS.

SO WHY DOES *MY* SPINE HAVE A *SIDEWAYS* BEND IN IT?

WELL JOHN, THERE ARE *THREE* POSSIBLE REASONS.

YOU MIGHT HAVE A PROBLEM WITH YOUR *BONES*,

YOU MIGHT HAVE A PROBLEM WITH YOUR *MUSCLES*.

AND SOMETIMES YOU CAN JUST BE A MEDICAL MYSTERY. NO-ONE KNOWS!

SOMETIMES WHEN YOU ARE BORN, THE *BONES* DON'T DEVELOP IN THE USUAL WAY--WHICH CAN MAKE YOUR SPINE LEAN OVER.

OTHER TIMES THE *MUSCLES* THAT HOLD YOUR SPINE STRAIGHT DON'T WORK PROPERLY. THIS CAN PULL YOUR SPINE INTO A BENDY SHAPE.

AND SOMETIMES, THE BONES AND MUSCLES ARE FINE. BUT YOUR SPINE JUST GROWS A BIT BENDY ANYWAY!

JUST BECAUSE YOUR SPINE DIDN'T GROW STRAIGHT DOESN'T MEAN IT'S NOT HEALTHY. IN FACT, BONE DOCTORS TRIED TO FIGURE OUT WHY HEALTHY SPINES CAN SOMETIMES BEND SIDEWAYS, AND THEY COULDN'T FIND ANY REASON AT ALL--IT JUST HAPPENS.

SO I'M JUST THE LUCKY ONE IN A MILLION?

HARDLY! ALTHOUGH SCOLIOSIS IS MUCH MORE COMMON IN GIRLS THAN BOYS, 2% OF KIDS AGED 16 HAVE SCOLIOSIS. THAT MEANS IN A HIGH SCHOOL OF 1000, 20 KIDS WILL HAVE SCOLIOSIS. IT'S QUITE COMMON. YOU'RE MORE LIKE A ONE IN FIFTY.

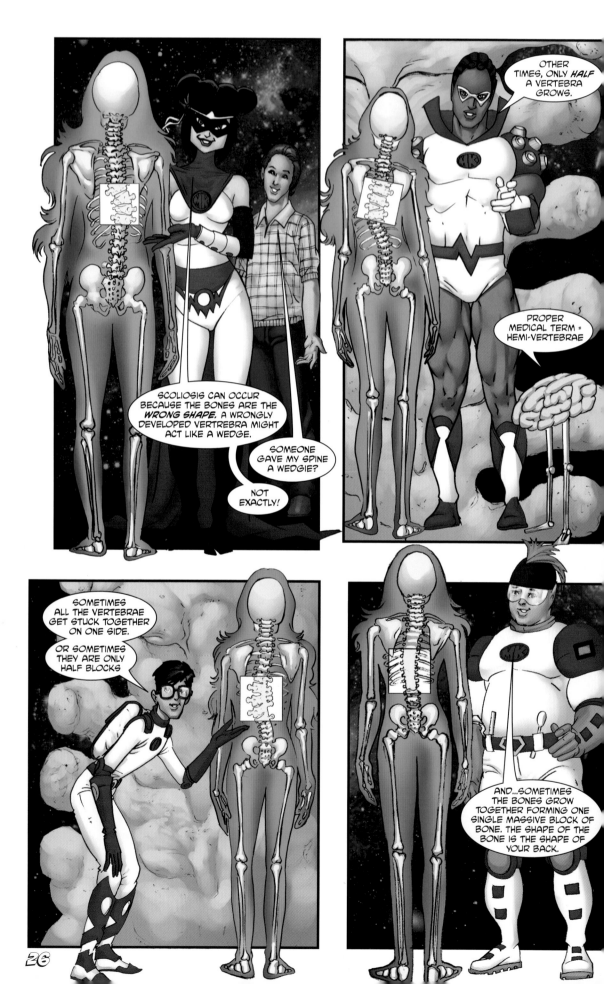